For James Pomerance — MM

For Tom and Elliot — AA

© 2009 by Orchard Books

This 2010 edition published by Sandy Creek,
by arrangement with Orchard Books.

Text © Margaret Mayo 2009
Illustrations © Alex Ayliffe 2009

Sandy Creek
122 Fifth Avenue
New York, NY 10011

ISBN: 978 1 4351 2842 2

A CIP catalogue record for this book
is available from the British Library.

Printed and bound in China
Manufactured April/2010

Lot 1   3   5   7   9   10   8   6   4   2

The rights of Margaret Mayo to be identified as the author
and Alex Ayliffe to be identified as illustrator of this work
have been asserted by them in accordance with the
Copyright, Designs and Patents Act, 1988.

Margaret Mayo & Alex Ayliffe
SNAP!

Sandy Creek

Sharks are good at **snap, snap, snapping,**
Whoosh! – dashing, tails **lashing,**
Spiky teeth ready for **snap, snapping.**
So **snap,** sharks, **snap!**

Dolphins are good at dance, dance, dancing,
High jumping, fast spinning,

Walrus are good at **waddle, waddle, waddling,**
As they huddle close, jostling, **wibble–wobbling,**

Making such a noise – blah! blah! – bellowing!
So waddle, walrus, waddle!

Whales are good at glide, glide, gliding,
Tails going up down, up down beating.

As they blast out air – **pouffe!** – tall spouts **creating.**

So **glide, whales, glide!**

Sea otters are good at float, float, floating.
Lying on their backs, shellfish scrunch, scrunching,

Little pups cradling and quietly snoozing.
So float, sea otters, float!

Penguins are good at dive, dive, diving, swooping, swerving, quick zig-zagging,

Tails and feet guiding, stiff wings **flip-flapping.**

So **dive, penguins, dive!**

Polar bears are good at **lollop, lollop, lolloping**

With cubs following · · ·

Slipping, sliding and **roly-polying!**
So **lollop**, polar bears, **lollop!**

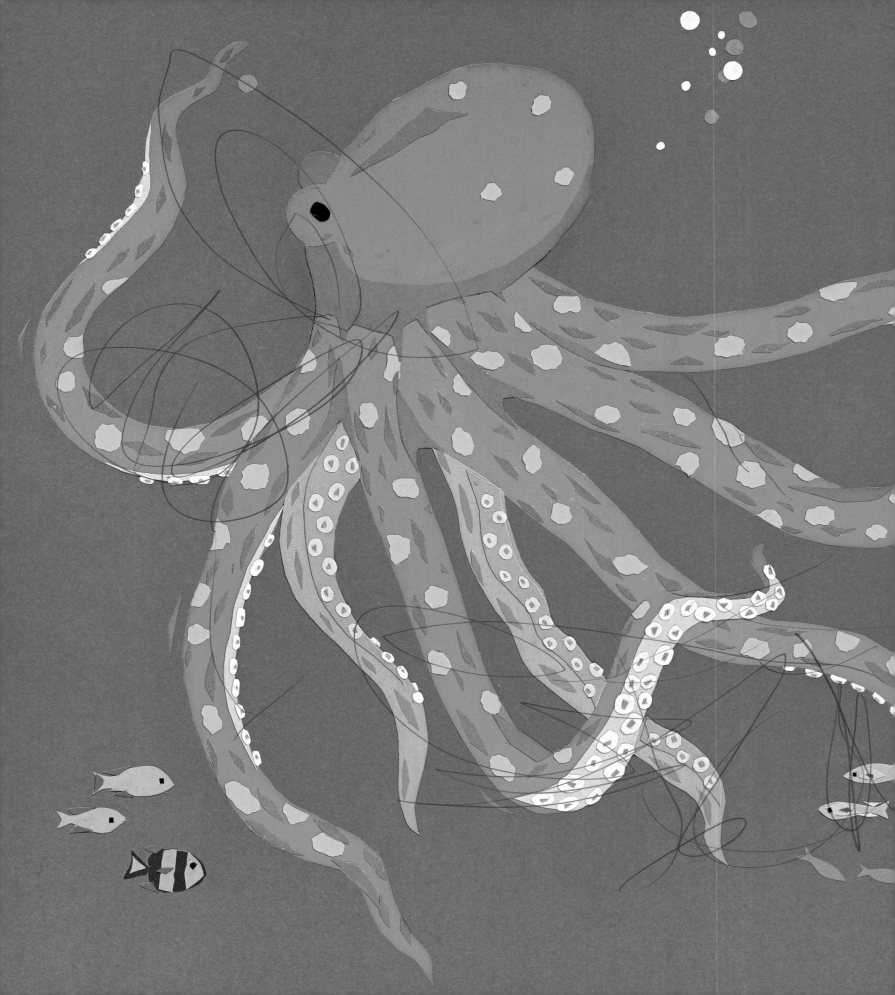

Octopuses are good at **waggle, waggle, waggling,**
Arms waving, food grabbing, **munch, munching,**
And – **squish!** – jetting off, long arms **trailing.**
So **waggle,** octopuses, **waggle!**

Stingrays are good at underwater **flying,**
Wide fins **sweeping,** ripple, **rippling,**

Spindly tails flicking and . . . stinging!
So fly, stingrays, fly!

Seals are good at **play, play, playing,** chasing, dodging and . . . ooohh! . . . somersaulting,

Coming to the surface and **snorting.**
So **play**, seals, **play!**

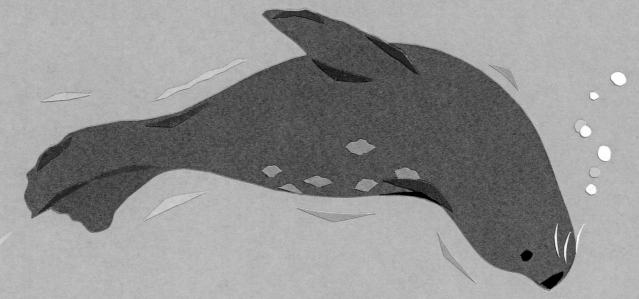

Sea turtles are good at **dig, dig, digging,**
Sand scoop scooping, safe nests **making,**

Eggs laying . . . more digging! . . . covering and hiding.

So dig, sea turtles, dig!

All these creatures are good at swimming,
But they can never live on the shore.

A snapping shark is one such creature.
Now look carefully – can you find some more?